THE LAST BOOK OF CATHOLIC JOKES

THE LAST BOOK OF CATHOLIC JOKES

Deacon Tom Sheridan
Foreword by Sister Mary Kathleen Glavich, SND

acta
PUBLICATIONS

THE LAST BOOK OF CATHOLIC JOKES
by Deacon Tom Sheridan
with a Foreword by Sister Mary Kathleen Glavich, SND

Edited by Gregory F. Augustine Pierce
Cover design by Tom A. Wright
Text design and typesetting by Patricia A. Lynch

Copyright © 2013 by Deacon Tom Sheridan

Published by ACTA Publications, 4848 N. Clark Street, Chicago, IL 60640, (800) 397-2282, www.actapublications.com

Library of Congress Catalog number: 2013953373
ISBN: 978-0-87946-522-3
Printed in the United States of America by United Graphics
Year 20 19 18 17 16 15 14 13
Printing 15 14 13 12 11 10 9 8 7 6 5 4 3 2 First

CONTENTS

DEDICATION

It was Auntie Mame who once wisely said that "life's a banquet and most poor suckers are starving to death." It's also true that life is full of opportunities for laughter and too many of us fail to see it. This final book of jokes poking gentle fun at our faith is dedicated to those who can appreciate the humor in their lives and in their faith. But it's also dedicated to those who cannot, with the hope that God will give them the gift of mirth.

This book must also be dedicated to Kathy, my wife of nearly five decades, who still thinks my sense of humor is a little, well, weird. Which, of course, it is.

FOREWORD

by Sister Mary Kathleen Glavich, SND

Why is a respected Catholic publishing house like ACTA Publications (which has published several of my books) producing joke books about Catholics? I think it is because jokes bring about joy, and joy happens to be one of the fruits of the Holy Spirit. In fact, according to the Jesuit Pierre Teilhard de Chardin, joy is the most infallible sign of the presence of God. Laughter has been called "carbonated holiness." With tongue in cheek, G. K. Chesterton wrote in his book *Orthodoxy*, "Angels can fly because they take themselves lightly" and "Satan fell by the force of gravity." We excel as human beings then when we imitate the angels (the good ones) by laughing at our own pretensions, prejudices, and peccadilloes — especially when it comes to our attempts to be "holy" and "religious."

Laughing isn't difficult. It's one of the first charming things babies do. Besides, humans like to laugh. That's why comedians and clowns are popular. Good public speakers, including homilists and catechists, spice their talks with humor to keep their audience laughing…and attentive. (Deacon Tom's books can keep them supplied with jokes for years!) My mother recalls that her family had a record with nothing on it but people laughing. Just for fun she and her nine siblings would play this record over and over, and — because laughter is contagious — they would all end up rolling on the floor with laughter.

As a man who is like us in all things except sin, Jesus must have enjoyed a good laugh too. Perhaps Mary taught her son the Jewish proverb, "What soap is to the body, laughter is to the soul." I can imagine Jesus seated with the apostles around a fire, swapping funny stories with them and maybe frowning a little (but not too much) when one of the disciples tells an off-color one! The Gospels give us glimpses of Jesus' sense of humor. He taught about a camel struggling to squeeze through a needle, a woman threatening to give a judge a black eye, and an oil lamp (!) placed under a bed. No doubt Jesus had a twinkle in his eye when he sent Peter, a fisherman, to find tax money in a fish's mouth.

It is sad that many people don't associate religion with laughter. They envision God as a stern judge watching to catch us doing wrong. To them, liturgy is a somber affair and giggling children ought to be banished to the crying room. They think that priests, deacons, brothers, and sisters are born without funny bones and that humor has no place in church. These misguided people apparently are unaware of St. Teresa of Avila's prayer: "From silly devotions and sour-faced saints, good Lord, deliver us!"

Lucky for us, Tom Sheridan is one deacon who knows the value of laughter. For the fourth (and last) time (he promises us), he has put together a collection of church-related jokes guaranteed to evoke hearty laughter or at least a smile from the most serious reader. In doing so, he doesn't spare us sisters, who are often the butt of Catholic jokes.

Even as a child I was familiar with the riddle "What's black and white and red all over? A nun rolling down a hill." On the day I entered the convent, my blood sister presented me with all black items, such as a black toothbrush! Very funny. Since then, I've received a magnet that shows two nuns in habits. One is asking the other, "So, what are you wearing tomorrow?" And each birthday I can expect at least one silly card with a nun-theme. Any day now someone will probably take delight in giving me one of those tee shirts that say, "You don't scare me. I was taught by nuns." Sometimes we sisters cringe at this kind of humor, but other times we can't help laughing ourselves, even to the point of tears.

One of the jokes about nuns in one of the previous books in this series is one that pokes fun at our driving. It went something like this:

A cop pulls over a carload of nuns. He says to the driver, "Sister, this is a 55 MPH highway. Why are you going so slow?"

The nun, who happened to be the Mother Superior, replies, "Sir, I saw a lot of signs that said 41, not 55."

The cop answers, "Oh, Sister, that's not the speed limit. It's the name of the highway you are on."

The Mother Superior says, "Silly me! Thanks for letting me know. I'll be more careful."

Then the cop looks in the backseat where three young postulates are cowering.

The cop asks, "Excuse me, Sister, what's wrong with your young friends back there? They are trembling something terrible."

The Mother Superior answers, "Oh, we just got off Highway 101 a few minutes ago."

Here (with apologies to all Sister Mary Roses) is a nun-joke Deacon Tom could not resist adding to this book:

Sister Mary Rose lived an exemplary life. When she died she was greeted at the Pearly Gates by St. Peter, who was clearly surprised to see her. He checked the records and said, "Sister, you're early; we weren't expecting you for some time yet. You'll have to return to earth and wait a while."

A week later, Sister Mary phoned heaven to bring St. Peter up to date. "This is Sister Mary Rose," she began, "and I just want to let you know that everything is fine. While I'm waiting, I rented a little apartment over a local bar and took a part-time job there."

St. Peter thanked her but told her it was still not time. "Give me another call in a few more weeks," he said.

Sister Mary phoned again in a month, asking St. Peter if she should come home yet. She told St. Peter that everything was still OK. In fact she had met some new friends and had even gone out dancing with a guy she had met at the bar. But St. Peter told her it still wasn't time. Another couple months went by and St. Peter got a brief text message: "Pete, this is Rose. Don't call me; I'll call you."

If you laughed at either of these jokes, you did your body a favor. Laughing is comparable to a good workout. Among other things it massages the liver, strengthens the immune system, improves circulation, and relaxes muscles. Laughter also releases endorphins, our feel-good hormones, and reduces stress, anger, depression, and anxiety. Musician and writer Jimmy Buffett once observed that if we couldn't laugh we would all go insane! No wonder laughter has been called part of the human survival kit.

So go ahead and take a dose of cheap medicine: Start reading this book.

This may be Tom Sheridan's last book of Catholic jokes, but don't you believe for one moment that we Catholics will ever stop laughing at the funny things we do and say.

THE <u>LAST</u> BOOK OF CATHOLIC JOKES

He — and, I know from being married nearly 50 years, she — who laughs last laughs best. That's an old maxim, which, like many other old maxims, is rooted in truth.

This is the fourth, and last, edition of *The Book of Catholic Jokes*. And I think it's the best. But I'm prejudiced. Then again, over the past several years I've had the experience of researching, rewriting, adapting, and in some cases warping thousands and thousands of jokes for this series of comical takes on the Catholic Church. I doubt there is a single joke even remotely about religion that I haven't heard.

In other words, it's time to say – in the language of the Church — *Satis satis est*. While the words are not exactly part of the Roman ritual, they are good Latin. The meaning is clear: Enough is enough!

Enough jokes, that is. Not enough laughing. There's never enough laughing.

Did you ever think about just how many jokes there are in the universe? How many little slices of humanity that tickle our funny bones? Must be millions. No, they aren't all in this book. But there are a couple of hundred. And these join the many hundreds of others that appear in the previous editions of *The Book of Catholic Jokes*.

We are a funny people. We manage to take human situations, turn them and twist them into little bits of comical human nature.

But jokes about religion? Why not? About people whose lives

are intertwined with their faith? You bet! Jokes about God? Certainly. (Don't worry, God has a great sense of humor; just consider the aardvark.)

And, yes, the jokes here are all clean. There are many more jokes about things religious in general or Catholics specifically that aren't so clean or are mean-spirited. You won't find any of those among these pages. Oh, you'll find some which poke a little good-natured fun at Catholic practices or stereotypical Catholic behavior, or even gently rib the Church's internal workings, but I assure you they are offered in the spirit of faith, hope, and love — and the greatest of these is love for the Church that has been and remains in my retirement an integral part of my life.

I'm frequently asked whether, after checking out so many thousands of jokes, and dozens of variations thereof, I have a favorite. Sorry, nope. But there are a couple from this edition that I especially chuckled at.

> *Several deacons and priests were traveling together by train to a clergy conference at Notre Dame University. Each of the priests had bought a ticket, but the deacons got together and bought a single ticket for them all.*
>
> *The priests were secretly hoping the deacons would get caught, but one of the deacons called out, "The conductor is coming," and the deacons all jumped up and squeezed into one of the toilets. The conductor punched the priests' tickets, and then noticed the toilet was occupied. He knocked on the door and said: "Ticket, please!" The deacons slid their single ticket under the door and the conductor continued merrily on his rounds.*

Heading home after the conference, the priests decided to use the same trick. They bought only one ticket, but they were baffled when they noticed the deacons didn't buy any tickets at all.

This time, when one deacon shouted, "The conductor is coming," the priests raced to the toilet and locked themselves in. The deacons leisurely walked to the other toilet in the car, but one of them, as he passed the priests' toilet, knocked on the door and said in an affected, officious voice, "Ticket, please!"

You see, the deacons…oh, never mind! Some jokes manage to allow us to look at our own human nature and gain an insight along with a chuckle. I was ordained a deacon a long time ago. Like many deacons, the first few years after ordination were a revelation and an opportunity. Perhaps sometimes too much of an opportunity. That's why this joke made me laugh, as well as ponder my own behavior. Here's another one.

Like many newly ordained deacons, John threw himself into parish activities and worked with abandon. He frequently told parishioners that if they wished a pastoral visit to just drop him an email and he would stop by.

One night, checking his email before yet another meeting, John received a note. It read, "I am one of your loneliest parishioners and biggest supporters. May I have a visit tomorrow evening?"

It was signed by his wife.

Finally, any worthy human organization — and the Catholic Church is indeed an organization run by humans who often do funny things – should be able to take itself with a grain of salt. Sort of like this:

> *When Jesus went into the region of Caesarea Philippi he asked his disciples, "Who do people say that the Son of Man is?" They replied, "Some say John the Baptist, others Elijah, still others Jeremiah or one of the prophets." He said to them, "But who do you say that I am?"*
>
> *Simon Peter said in reply, "Master, you are the supreme eschatological manifestation of omnipotent ecclesiastical authority, the absolute, divine and sacerdotal monarch."*
>
> *And Jesus said, "Huh?"*

So, dear reader, enough is enough. Enjoy this *Last Book of Catholic Jokes* and take one more moment to laugh a little at ourselves.

Deacon Tom Sheridan
Ocala, Florida

THE JOKES

The crusty old monsignor took over a very large parish with many staff members. He called them all together soon after his installation and presented some fairly radical plans for changing how things were done in the parish, knowing that several of the staff would disagree.

Sure enough, several did — vociferously.

"Well, we're going to run this parish collegially," he told the staff. "All in favor of my new plans, say 'Aye.' All opposed, say 'I resign.'"

The newly ordained deacon was certain he'd found his true calling. He wanted to spend every last minute at the church, praying and taking on more and more duties. Finally, he realized his ministry was being held back by his "real" job. Thinking it over, he came up with a plan.

One evening, before heading back to the church for yet another meeting, he told his wife, "I found a great new job. The pay is wonderful, benefits tremendous, and offers three weeks' vacation."

"That does sound great," she said.

"That's good," he said. "You start tomorrow."

The perennially overworked and underpaid parish secretary stomped into the pastor's office and in no uncertain terms demanded a raise. "I do a good job for this church and you should know there are three organizations that are trying almost every day to hire me away from here," she told him.

"Really?" said the pastor, surprised. "What three organizations?"

"The phone company, the gas company and the electric company," she said, "They want to hire me to head up their church collection departments."

She got the raise.

The parish's youth minister went to the pastor and told him, "Can I have tomorrow off? My wife wants me to rearrange all the furniture, clean the floors, and paint the garage."

The pastor looked over the schedule and saw that the school had a retreat planned. "We're really too busy tomorrow; I can't give you the day off," he said.

"Gee, thanks, Father," said the youth minister, smiling. "I knew I could count on you."

The young associate pastor was very pleased. It was his first assignment at a busy suburban parish. Why, he even had a real nice office all his own. Sitting there behind his shiny new desk he felt really important. When he spotted a man coming in he wanted to seem busy so he picked up his phone and pretended to have a conversation.

At last he hung up the phone and asked the man who was waiting patiently to see him, "Can I help you?"

"You bet," said the man. "I'm here to hook up your phone."

The brother, newly assigned as a missionary in the Alaskan backcountry, was full of fervor for the Word of God.

He was confident that he, and God, could handle anything the wilderness could throw at him. He spotted a local guide and said smugly, "I know that carrying this big lantern will keep the grizzly bears away."

"You might be right," said the guide. "But only if you carry it real fast."

The deacon was such a mild soul that you'd think he'd hardly hurt a flea. Still, he loved duck hunting. One day, after a long wet morning in the marsh he had nothing to show for his efforts. Still dressed in his camouflage hunting gear, he slipped into the local butcher shop. He asked the butcher, "Say, can I get a couple of ducks?"

"No ducks today," said the butcher. "But I can give you a couple of nice chickens."

"Chickens," shouted the deacon. "I can't tell my wife I shot a couple of chickens! Give me a side of beef. I'll tell her I shot a cow."

———

The pastor was interviewing a young man for the job of director of the parish's youth ministry. "Remember," he told the man, "we care a great deal about cleanliness here and it's something we want to teach our young people. Did you wipe your feet on the mat before coming in the door?"

"Absolutely," said the candidate.

The pastor looked at him and said, "We also want to teach our youth about honesty here. There is no mat at the door."

The old pastor knew how to run a parish. But he didn't know a thing about machines. One evening the newly minted associate, fresh from his ordination, was walking by the office and spotted the pastor standing in front of the shredder, befuddled. He held a piece of paper in his hand.

"Can you help me?" he asked the associate. "This is an extremely sensitive document and the secretary has already left. I need this done right away."

Seeing a chance to get himself in the good graces of his new boss, the young associate said, "No problem, Father," snatched the paper from the pastor's hand, slipped it into the machine, and pressed "start."

"Wonderful," said the pastor as the shredder chopped away. "I just need one copy."

The catechist was in the middle of a lesson when she asked the class, "Who is God?"

From the back row, Little Jonnie's voice spoke out: "God is our chauffeur."

"What makes you say that, Jonnie?" asked the catechist.

"Well," said the sixth grader, "he drove Adam and Eve out of the Garden of Eden, didn't he?"

The parish's marriage enrichment ministry program usually included a brief story and lesson from Scripture. This week, the presenters told the story of Abraham and Sarah who, though in their 90s, were blessed by God with a child.

"What can we learn from their experience?" the presenter asked the group.

The husband of a young couple who were struggling financially blurted out, "Well, at least they waited until they could afford the kid."

The Catholic school teacher was joking with her class and asked, "What does God do for a living?"

"That's easy," said Little Janie. "He's a painter. Just look at all the beauty in the world!"

"That's a very creative thought, Janie," said the teacher. The world is certainly a piece of art."

"And God paints using only his left hand," Janie continued.

Perplexed, about all the teacher could respond was, "Why, Janie, whatever do you mean? Why do you think that God only uses his left hand?"

"Because you told us Jesus was sitting on his right hand."

The night was dark and the Catholic Marine on guard duty was having a hard time staying awake. He jarred himself awake several times, but finally gave in and fell asleep. With a start, he opened his eyes to find the camp chaplain, a full colonel, standing in front of him. Thinking quickly, the Marine quickly lowered his head again and said loudly, "Amen!"

The Wall Street investor wasn't a regular churchgoer, but when he needed help finding the cash to close a big deal he figured a little prayer couldn't hurt. He stopped in St. Patrick's Cathedral on his lunch hour and by chance ended up next to a poor man who was praying out loud for money. Only this fellow wanted just $20 to pay off a small debt.

The investor overheard the guy's prayer, opened his wallet, and peeled off a $20 bill. His prayer answered, the man thanked him and rushed out of the pew.

The investor then prayed, "Lord, now that I have your undivided attention…"

Remember the Scripture about Lot's wife,
who looked back and turned into a pillar of salt?

She had nothing on the priest who looked back
while driving and turned into a light pole.

The Catholic mom was teaching her young son, Little Jonnie, how to pray. One afternoon, as she was taking him to McDonald's for a treat, they passed by a fender-bender in the road. It didn't seem serious, but the mother told her son that they should always pray for accident victims.

She prayed for the well-being of those involved in the accident. As she finished, Little Jonnie piped in: "And God, please don't let there be an accident at the entrance to McDonald's."

———

The rich Catholic man always said the secret to his financial success was found in using *Lectio Divina* with the Bible.

"For example," he said, "I opened the Good Book and pointed to a word. It was 'oil,' so I invested in oil and the gushers came in. Then I did it again and the word was 'gold,' and I bought some gold stock and the mines produced and produced."

But one day the man had a financial setback. So he opened his Bible and pointed to the page. The words read, "Chapter Eleven."

———

Fashion is always an important item at weddings. As the bride processed down the aisle, a guest asked, "Doesn't the bride look stunning?"

"She sure does," responded her mate. "And doesn't the groom look stunned."

The priest was a great guy, but he had a heavy foot. One Sunday morning he was on his way to the church for Mass when he was pulled over by a cop for speeding. As the cop checked his license and registration, car after car passed along the road with the drivers honking and waving.

Finally the cop asked the priest what was going on. "I'm pastor of the church down the street," he said, "which is where I was heading when you stopped me. My parishioners all recognized me."

The cop chuckled and stopped writing the ticket. "No fine this time, Father," he said. "I think your parishioners will punish you enough when you shake their hands on the way out of Mass!"

During his summer vacation, the new Catholic high school teacher injured his back and had to wear a fiberglass cast under his shirt around his upper body.

On the first day of school he was having a hard time keeping the boys, especially Little Jonnie, quiet. So he opened a window until a breeze made his tie flap over his shoulder. Then he walked calmly over to his desk, picked up a big stapler, and stapled the tie to his chest.

No boy in the class, even Little Jonnie, was ever inattentive again.

The rectory's new housekeeper was a great cook, but she lacked in a few other areas. One day she answered the phone as she was cleaning the office and said, "That's right!" It rang again almost immediately and the housekeeper answered it: "Yes, it certainly is." This went on twice more with similar results before the pastor, who had been listening to all this, asked who had called.

"I have no idea," the housekeeper replied. "Someone kept saying, 'It's a long-distance from Rome,' and I agreed with them."

A deacon and wife went to a potluck supper at their parish. After a while, the man scolded his wife saying, "I don't believe it; that's the third time you've hit the dessert table. Everyone will think you're a glutton."

"No, they won't," she replied with a smirk. "I've been telling people they're for you."

The pastor asked the parish bookkeeper and the head of the parish council for their opinion on the parish financial situation.

"Well," said the pair, "our financial situation is very fluid."

"And what exactly does that mean?" asked the pastor.

"We're going down the drain."

The IRS was auditing the pizza shop owner, a very devout Catholic. The agent wanted to know how the man could justify deducting trips to Rome, Fatima, Lourdes and the Holy Land in a single year.

"We deliver," he said with a shrug.

After getting a traffic ticket, the young woman found herself in court. The judge asked what she did for a living. The woman replied proudly, "I'm a teacher at St. Mary's Catholic School."

"In that case," said the judge, "I have the perfect punishment, one I've been waiting since I went to Catholic school myself to give. Sit down at that table and write 'I will never run a stop sign again' 200 times before you go home."

The teacher laughed and said, "And I suppose you expect me to use the Palmer method for my handwriting!"

The two women were getting acquainted at a Catholic Charities employees' meeting. The first introduced herself and said, "You know, I live off the spat of the land."

The second woman replied, "Surely you mean the fat of the land, don't you?"

"No," said the first woman, "I mean spat. I'm the marriage counselor here."

**The two seminarians had completed a basic class
in pastoral counseling the previous week.
One afternoon they met on the street and greeted each other:
"You're fine; how am I?"**

The Catholic missionary had spent decades in the bush working with doctors to heal natives' illnesses. Now he had come home and was looking forward to his assignment as pastor of a nice suburban parish. At the beginning of his first staff meeting, he startled everyone by walking into the room shouting, "Measles! Whooping cough! Tetanus! Typhoid!"

"What's up with that," the music director asked the secretary.

"Nothing, really," she replied. "He just wants everyone to know he calls the shots around here."

After describing the beauty of the heavenly afterlife to her second-grade class, the catechist asked the children, "All right, how many of you want to go to heaven?"

Little Janie immediately piped up, "I can't. I promised Mom I'd come right home after school."

The members of Boy Scout Troop 34 from St. Mary's Cathedral were a bunch of city guys, but they thought they were tough and ready for anything on their first camping trip in the woods.

But after the sun set they found that country mosquitoes were much more ferocious than their urban cousins. It got so bad that the scouts pulled their blankets over their heads to keep from being eaten alive. The parish's youth minister was covered up like the rest but he peeked out of his blanket long enough to spot several lightning bugs darting around the campfire.

"OK, guys, we gotta give up," he called out to his scouts. "They're using flashlights now!"

The new director of the youth choir had worked with the kids for months, preparing them for their first appearance at Mass. The children were nervous; so was the director.

So right before the Mass, she told them that if they weren't sure of their part they should just pretend to sing and mouth the words instead.

Finally, the Mass started and the director brought her hand down to start the opening hymn.

She was, of course, met with complete silence.

The new deacon was invited to give a talk on Scripture at the parish's adult education program. However, the afternoon before the talk, the maintenance staff removed all the chairs from the parish hall to clean the floor.

When the audience arrived, there were no chairs and it was too late to set them all up again. So everyone stood while the deacon gave his presentation.

When he returned home his wife asked how the evening went.

"Wonderful!" he said. "Every seat in the house was taken before I even got there and the audience gave me a standing ovation throughout my talk!"

The parish support group for mothers-to-be was very popular. There were lots of good tips about preparing for the blessed event, especially about staying healthy during pregnancy.

One night the instructor was explaining how beneficial walking was for pregnant women. She told the men that they should encourage walking as an exercise. "You could even go with her," the instructor said.

One of the men shouted, "Would it be OK if she carries a golf bag while we walk?"

One Sunday, returning from receiving Communion, a woman asked the man at the end of the pew, "Excuse me, did I step on your foot when I left?"

The man, obviously expecting an apology, replied curtly, "Yes, you did."

The woman smiled and said, "Good. Then this is my pew."

After a successful career in business, a man discerned that he had a late vocation and entered the seminary. After ordination he was assigned to a parish. One Saturday afternoon he was about to hear confessions when he met an old friend from his former life.

"How do you like the new job?" the friend asked.

"Well," said the new priest, "The pay's not so good and the hours are long." Then, pointing to the confessional, he said, "But what I do like is that in this business, the customer is always wrong!"

The pastor had hoped he wouldn't have to talk with the associate about his frequent disappearances from their Chicago parish. But he finally called the young priest into his office and said, "Father, I have noticed that every time the Cubs are playing a day game at home your aunt becomes ill and you have to take her to the doctor."

The associate looked at the pastor and replied innocently, "You're right, Father. You don't think she's faking it, do you?"

Several deacons and priests were traveling together by train to a clergy conference at Notre Dame University. Each of the priests had bought a ticket, but the deacons got together and bought a single ticket for them all.

The priests were secretly hoping the deacons would get caught, but one of the deacons called out, "The conductor is coming," and the deacons all jumped up and squeezed into one of the toilets. The conductor punched the priests' tickets, and then noticed the toilet was occupied. He knocked on the door and said: "Ticket, please!" The deacons slid their single ticket under the door and the conductor continued merrily on his rounds.

Heading home after the conference, the priests decided to use the same trick. They bought only one ticket, but they were baffled when they noticed the deacons didn't buy any tickets at all.

This time, when one deacon shouted, "The conductor is coming," the priests raced to the toilet and locked themselves in. The deacons leisurely walked to the other toilet in the car, but one of them, as he passed the priests' toilet, knocked on the door and said in an affected, officious voice, "Ticket, please!"

"Do you know who built the ark?

"No, uh…"

"Why, that's correct!"

The two retired Catholic military chaplains living in a home for elderly priests had spent their lives in service to their God and their country — one in the U.S. Marines, the other in the U.S. Navy. They were sitting around the parlor one day having a good-natured argument about who had it rougher.

The Marine chaplain said proudly, "I did 30 years with the Corps. I hit the beach at Okinawa with my men, clawed my way up the blood-soaked sand, and prayed side by side with them as they fought and died. I was in Korea with General MacArthur, freezing along with the troops. Finally, I served in Vietnam, crawling through the mud and razor grass for 14 hours a day, plagued by rain and mosquitoes, ducking under sniper fire all day and mortar fire all night."

"Ah," said the old Navy Chaplain with a dismissive wave of his hand, "all shore duty, huh?"

During a parish-sponsored retreat in the Rocky Mountains, two laymen were wandering in the bush near their lodge when one spotted a huge grizzly bear.

Both men quickly dropped to their knees. But rather than praying for salvation, one started to quickly put on a pair of running shoes. His friend said, "Are you nuts? You can't outrun a grizzly bear!"

"True enough," said the man. "But I only have to outrun you."

During the first session with a new couple about to get married, the marriage prep team had the engaged couple fill out a premarital inventory questionnaire.

As the couple answered the list questions separately, they both came to one that asked, "Are you entering this marriage of your own free will?"

Before the soon-to-be husband could answer, his future wife leaned over and whispered, "Say 'yes.'"

Q: How come Moses didn't fish while he was on the ark?

A: Moses was never on the ark.

**Q: O.K. Then how come Noah didn't fish
while he was on the ark?**

A: He only had two worms.

After Mass one Sunday, as two girls were leaving church, they walked past the parish's deacon. "Goodbye, Father," said one.

The other said, "He's no father, you dummy. He's married with four kids."

St. Peter looked up from his duties guarding heaven's gate and saw an amazing sight. Coming along together were the Pope and Frankenstein. Peter checked his book quickly and discovered, to his shock, that heaven was nearly full. In fact, there was room for only one more entry that day.

Without hesitation, Peter waved Frankenstein into heaven and told the Pope he'd have to wait until the next day for an opening.

The Pope was shocked and demanded to know why.

"Well," said St. Peter, "to be honest, Your Holiness, that monster scared the hell out of more people than you ever did."

———

At the parish's monthly pre-baptism class, the deacon asked the group of parents, "Name two things that the Church says are required for baptism."

From the back of the room came a voice: "Water and a baby."

———

Just as he was about to baptize the baby, the deacon intoned the words of the baptismal rite: "What name do you give this child?"

The father spoke up and proudly said, "John Thomas James Reginald Carl Winters IV."

The deacon looked over at the altar boy and whispered, "Get more water."

It was the early Mass on Sunday morning. The day was bright and warm, just right for golf. Father muttered to the altar servers just before the opening procession. "Bet we've got lots of golfers here this morning," he said.

"How do you know who they are?" replied one of the servers.

"Just watch their hands when they pray," Father responded. "They all use an interlocking grip."

The deacon's ministry was to make pastoral visits to the local hospital's mental ward. As he was visiting the rooms, one patient came up to him and said, "Good morning, Deacon. I'm God."

The deacon decided to play along and said, "Nice to meet you, God. You know, I was wondering about…"

The man waved his hand dismissively and said, "Sorry, son, not on my day off."

The piano tuner came into the church one afternoon and spoke to the music director. "I'm here to tune your piano," he said.

"But," stammered the musician, "I didn't call you."

"That's true," said the tuner. "But several of your parishioners did."

Sister Mary Rose lived an exemplary life. When she died she was greeted at the Pearly Gates by St. Peter, who was clearly surprised to see her. He checked the records and said, "Sister, you're early; we weren't expecting you for some time yet. You'll have to return to earth and wait a while."

A week later, Sister Mary phoned heaven to bring St. Peter up to date. "This is Sister Mary Rose," she began, "and I just want to let you know that everything is fine. While I'm waiting, I rented a little apartment over a local bar and took a part-time job there."

St. Peter thanked her but told her it was still not time. "Give me another call in a few more weeks," he said.

Sister Mary phoned again in a month, asking St. Peter if she should come home yet. She told St. Peter that everything was still OK. In fact she had met some new friends and had even gone out dancing with a guy she had met at the bar. But St. Peter told her it still wasn't time.

Another couple months went by and St. Peter got a brief text message: "Pete, this is Rose. Don't call me; I'll call you."

"Well, how'd it go?" asked the deacon's wife as he returned from celebrating his first wedding.

"It went OK," responded the deacon, "until we came to the part in the vows about the wife being obedient to her husband. That's when the bride answered, 'Do you think I'm nuts?' and the groom said, 'I do.' It all went downhill from there."

A Chicago priest was deep in prayer one night when sudden-ly God responded and said God would answer three questions.

The priest thought and asked whether people around the world would learn to live peacefully together. "Yes," God replied, "but not in your lifetime."

He thought again and asked, "Will all people ever come to know the presence of God in their lives? "Yes," God replied, "but not in your lifetime."

At last, the priest asked the question he'd held deep in his heart for decades. "God," he asked, "will the Chicago Cubs ever win the World Series?"

God pondered for a moment and replied. "Yes," God said finally. "But not in my lifetime."

The parish needed a new church building since the old one was literally falling down. The pastor was preaching about the need to support the building fund and asked the parishioners to pledge one-tenth of their income to the fund.

One cheapskate in the back pew was heard muttering to his wife, "Let's not give. They'll only want more. I'll bet they'll be asking for one-twentieth next."

Margaret was a saintly woman who never missed the opportunity for the sacrament of penance. She was, however, also very forgetful. Which is why she arrived at the confessional with her sins, minor though they were, listed neatly on a piece of paper.

Rather than announce her sins loudly — being a bit deaf, Margaret had a tendency to shout — she would just hand the list to her confessor. On one particular Saturday, however, Margaret handed over the list and the priest looked at it and said, "What's this? It looks like a grocery list."

Margaret snatched the list back, looked at it, and gasped. "Oh my God," she bellowed. "I left my sins at the supermarket!"

———

It was a terrible accident. A bus carrying the ladies of the Rosary and Altar Society crashed and all were killed. In heaven, St. Peter was distraught because there wasn't enough room for them, as the new addition wasn't quite finished. He quickly made a deal with Satan for the ladies to stay in hell until the work was completed.

A few days later, Satan called St. Peter, exasperated. "I can't keep these ladies here any longer; you have to get them out."

"What's wrong?' asked Peter.

Satan responded, "Between their bake sales and bingo they've already raised enough to air-condition this place."

An insufferably pious bishop and one of his priests were playing golf. The priest was having a very bad day. Every ball he hit ended up in the rough or a sand trap or a water hazard. And every time it happened, the priest would utter a mild curse. After each incident of this, the bishop would admonish the priest. "You keep swearing like that and God will punish you, Father," he warned. "You should be like me and offer up your misfortunes to the Lord, who will certainly repay you a hundredfold."

But on the very next hole, the priest sliced the ball into a pond. He slammed his club down and shouted, "Missed again, doggone it!"

"Now, Father," the bishop said, "remember what I said. God will punish you for your sins. You need to become more holy, like me."

Just then, a bolt of white lightning burst from the clouds and hit the bishop squarely on the head.

A deep voice bellowed from the clouds, "Doggone it! Missed again!"

——

On Vatican Airlines, the pilot gives emergency instructions in Latin. It's so conservatives know how to get off the plane in case of a crash-landing.

On the other hand, the magazine in the seat pockets is in English. It's so liberals can read something written by the Curia since Vatican II.

The man arrived for his counseling session with the Catholic Charities therapist. As he sat in the waiting room, the receptionist watched as the man waved his arms over his head every couple of minutes.

She was used to unusual behavior in the office, but this was the first time she had seen this particular action. After several energetic episodes of the man's waving, she finally asked him: "Is there a fly that's bothering you?"

"No, Ma'am," the patient replied.

"Then, what's with all the waving?" she asked.

"Well," he said, looking around. "It keeps the vultures away."

The receptionist chuckled and said, "There are no vultures in this office."

"You're welcome," said the man.

———

At home after Mass, the couple was shocked to see Little Jonnie pull out handfuls of coins – nickels, dimes and quarters – from his pockets.

"Where did you get that money?" they asked him.

"At church," Jonnie answered. "They passed around baskets of it."

"Why did you only take the change?" his parents asked him.

"That's all they had in there," Jonnie explained.

Little Janie came home from religious education class and proudly announced that she had learned the Lord's Prayer. But she had a question.

"Mommy," she asked sweetly, "if we get our daily bread from God, why do we need bakeries?"

———

The choir was just awful one Sunday before Easter. It was clear they were struggling.

A man turned to his wife during one particularly bad song and said, "The music director must have given up melody for Lent."

———

At an ecumenical service at St. Mary's one evening, the pastor remarked just before the collection, "We welcome all denominations here. But we especially favor tens, twenties, and fifties."

———

During a remodeling project, St. Joseph's installed hot-air hand dryers in the church restrooms. They were removed a week later — right after the pastor discovered a sign taped to one of the dryers. It read, "To hear a recording of this week's homily, press here."

The pastor asked a sign-maker in the parish to donate a big sign for the sanctuary for Christmas Mass.

"Now, do it exactly as I have written it on this piece of paper," the priest ordered the man. "And make sure you have it up in time!"

Sure enough, as people walked into church for Christmas Mass they found this banner: "Unto us a child is born. Ten feet long and three feet wide."

———

The deacon was preaching a homily at a special celebration for the parish's children. The kiddies were all gathered up around the altar while the beaming parents sat in the pews.

The deacon was inspired by the church's beautiful stained-glass windows which recounted several stories from the Bible. As he spoke, he reminded the children that it took many different panels of glass to tell the story. And then he said, "Each of you is like one of those panels." Pointing to each of the children, he said, "You're a little pane; you're a little pane, you're a little…"

———

Plaque on the wall of St. Thomas parish:
"The loudspeaker was donated by John Jones
in memory of his wife."

The parish's custodian began noticing an unusual thing. Each Sunday after Mass there were brown bags being left in the pews. It began with a few, but in a couple of weeks there were many. After checking out a few of the bags, the custodian went directly to the pastor and said, "You might want to cut down your homilies, Father. People are beginning to bring their lunch."

The small parish's roof leaked and the pastor was trying to get a better bid to fix it. "Can't you do it for less?" He pleaded with the contractor, who was a member of the parish. "I'm just a poor country preacher."

"Don't I know it," said the contractor. "I heard your homily last week."

On Sunday following Mass at Holy Family Church, an inconsiderate smoker tossed a butt into some shrubbery. The priest spotted the bush smoldering and immediately called 911.

"Wait a minute, Father," the dispatcher said, "You're telling me there's a burning bush in front of your church and you want us to put it OUT?"

**Sign on the newly mopped floor of St. Mary's Parish Hall:
"Please do not walk on the water."**

St. Paul's was a rural parish. That meant that sometimes earthly chores had to take precedence over heavenly ones.

"Sometimes it's better to spread a load of manure and think about the Scriptures rather than listen to a homily about the Scriptures and think about spreading manure," seemed to be the motto of some of the farmers.

St. Mary's was deep in coal-mining country. One day, talking with the parish's teen group, the pastor remarked, "Remember, boys and girls, faith can move mountains."

One boy, the son of a miner, replied, "But dynamite sure is more exciting."

Right there in the middle of the priest's homily, a man in the second pew just got up and walked out the door.

After Mass, his wife went up to the priest and apologized. "I hope it didn't upset you too much," she said. "But please don't take it personally. My husband's been walking in his sleep for years."

Moses was sitting by himself when the Lord spoke to him.

"Moses," God said, "I have good news and bad news."

"You'd better give me the good news first," said Moses.

"OK," said God. "The good news is that I have chosen you to lead my people from slavery. Pharaoh will free the Jews because I will release plagues of locusts and frogs and cause devastation upon Egypt. Then you will lead my people across the Red Sea, which I will part for you."

"But Lord," asked Moses, "how could there possibly be any bad news after all that?"

"Well, my son," God said, "you will first have to fill out all the environmental impact forms."

———

**Scripture tells us a great paradox:
We should love both our neighbors and our enemies.**

Often they are the same people.

———

Sylvia was your typical old church lady — but with one difference. She was addicted to soap operas.

It got so bad that when one of the characters on the show got sick she put his name on the parish prayer list.

The discussions at the weekly Bible study sessions were usually pretty good. This week, the group was talking about death and how they would spend their last two weeks if they knew they were going to die.

One member said she'd spend the time witnessing about Jesus to her neighbors. Another said he'd do volunteer work to leave the world in a better way. But one man had a different idea.

"Here's what I'd do," he told the group. "I'd get the smallest car I could find and for two weeks I'd drive me and my mother-in-law around the country. Each night we'd stay in a cheap motel and order in fast food."

The group was stunned. They asked him, "Why would you choose to do that?"

"Because," said the man, "it would make them seem like the longest two weeks of my life and like they would never end. And at the end, I'd be ready to die."

When St. Monica's parish built its new church, the parish council decided to move the beautiful old organ from the old building to the new one, saving the cost of a replacement. Since the old organ had quite a long history, it became quite newsworthy.

Finally the delicate task was completed. The newspaper headline, however, left many dismayed: "St. Monica Gets Organ Transplant."

Did you hear about the accident involving the new priest with the "holier-than-thou" attitude?

No, what happened?

He was out walking his pet duck on the lake and a motorboat ran over him.

The visiting lecturer was struggling to explain to the parish adult education class the differences between some of the Protestant denominations.

"Put it this way," he finally said. "A Methodist is a Baptist who's afraid of water; a Presbyterian is a Baptist who went to college; and an Episcopalian is a Baptist whose business was successful."

The newly ordained deacon was proud of his preaching and worked very hard on his homilies. Late on Saturday evening after he had prepared his homily, he discovered that his dog ate the only copy of his notes.

He was devastated. That Sunday he stepped into the pulpit and confessed to the congregation.

"I had a great homily for you this morning, but since my dog chewed it up I'm going to have to rely on the inspiration of the Lord today," he said. "But I promise to do better next week."

The public school teacher entered his classroom a little early one morning and was shocked to discover several of his students on their knees in a corner.

"Just what do you think you're doing?" he demanded.

One of the boys shouted back, "We're playing craps."

"Thank God," he replied. "I was afraid you were praying."

The group of regulars were knocking back brews one evening at their neighborhood drinking establishment when the conversation turned to religion, specifically the selection of the new pope, which was then in process.

Nursing his beer, one of the guys finally said, "Y'know, the Catholics have had it long enough; I hope a Lutheran gets it this time."

Q: How many soloists does it take to change a light bulb?

A: Just one, but he'll need six weeks to prepare and will be upset if his name is spelled wrong in the program.

One Sunday afternoon, two friends were talking about the Mass that day; one had been, the other had not. "So, what did the pastor preach about today?" the second one asked.

"I'm not sure," the first replied. "He never said."

The deacon had a bit of an ego. A little too much. One Sunday, after delivering what he thought was a great homily, he was pretty full of himself. On the way home from church he asked his wife, "So, how many great preachers do you think there are in this town?"

She replied with a grin, "One less than you think."

After Mass his mother asked Little Jonnie how he had liked church that day.

"The music was fine," Jonnie replied. "But the commercial was too long."

If all the people who sleep in church were laid end to end, they'd be more comfortable.

At least until the line made it all the way around the globe and they began to double up.

The pastor was a great guy, but he had a reputation for long and boring homilies. Nothing could get him to change. Finally one Sunday, following a particularly tedious talk, he announced to his parishioners, "You know, I don't mind you people looking at your watches while I'm preaching, but it does bother me when you shake them to see if they're still running. It bothers me even more when you check your smartphones to see what day it is."

———

The new associate pastor came with some pretty high-falutin' credentials. In addition to the expected theology degrees, he had a B.S. in accounting, an M.S. in business, and a Ph.D. in psychology.

The old-school pastor thought it was time to take the new guy down a peg or two. He said to the associate, "Son, I know what B.S. is. M.S. means more of the same. And Ph.D. just means piled higher and deeper."

———

The pastor's sermon was powerful and thoughtful. After Mass, several parishioners told him how good they thought it was. But one woman came up and said, "Father, every homily you preach is better than the next one."

Gladys was a conceited woman. And she knew it. One day, she was talking with the pastor after a church meeting and said, "Father, this morning I spent almost an hour just looking in the bedroom mirror admiring myself and thinking how beautiful I was. Do I have to confess that and do penance?"

"Actually, no," the priest said after thinking for a moment. "You only have to confess sins, not errors in judgment."

The publisher of the archdiocese's weekly newspaper was canvassing the town in search of ads for his paper. He'd managed to sign up most of the businesses, but he never could persuade the owner of the town's only general store to buy.

"Nope," the proprietor told him again. "As long as I've been here, I've never had to advertise."

"Well," drawled the publisher, pointing to a tall building down the street, "can you tell me what that place is?"

"That's St. John's Cathedral," said the store owner, chuckling. "You know that."

"Of course," the publisher replied. "Tell me, has it been there long?"

"Yup," said the owner, "almost a century."

"And," said the publisher, "they still ring their bell to remind people they're still there."

The store owner signed up that day.

The pastor came to St. Mary's right after ordination and stayed for many years. He became very popular with the parishioners. Finally he was being reassigned. There was a huge party in the parish hall acknowledging his years of service. During the celebration, a woman came up to wish him well.

"I'm sorry you're leaving. I just don't know what we'll do without you," she said. "Until you came to St. Mary's we didn't even know what sin was."

———

The pastor was trying to introduce a little Bible instruction at the parish's annual Men's Club meeting. He asked one old guy who was sitting in the back of the room trying to hide, "What story in the Bible do you like the best?"

The man pondered a bit and replied, "The one about the guy who loafs and fishes."

———

Q: Why did Mary and Joseph take Jesus with them when they went to Egypt and later to Jerusalem?

A: They couldn't afford a babysitter.

Catching some rays on a warm spring day, the priest was sitting directly behind a statue of Mary in the parish yard.

The parish school was just letting out and Little Janie came by and stopped at the front of the statue. "Oh, Virgin Mary," she prayed. "Can I bring Jan to the parish picnic in June? She's not a Catholic, you know, but she's my best friend."

Unseen, the priest listened intently to the girl's plea. Then he spoke from behind the statue in his deep voice. "I'm sorry, but the picnic is for parishioners only."

Little Janie was undaunted. "You be quiet, Jesus," she said crossly. "I'm talking to your mother."

The religion class was preparing for the sacrament of reconciliation. The teacher finally asked, "And what must we do before our sins can be forgiven?"

"That's easy," piped Little Jonnie from the back of the room. "First, we have to sin."

The interfaith clergy meeting had degenerated into an argument about which religion was better. Finally, the Catholic monsignor, who never did have much use for such gatherings in the first place, said they should all agree to disagree. "You worship God in your way," he told the group. "And I'll worship him in His way."

The deacon was pretty proud of his homilies. (Probably too proud, but that's another story.)

After spotting one of his neighbors at Mass one Sunday, he said, "Nice to see you at Mass again. Is it because of my homilies?"

"Nope," replied the friend. "It's because of my wife's preaching if I don't go to church."

———

It was the young priest's first homily. As soon as Mass was over he rushed into the sacristy to ask the pastor: "Well, Father, did I put enough fire into my homily?"

The pastor looked at him kindly and said, "You bet, Father. Only I wonder if it would have been better to put some of your homily into the fire instead."

———

The pastor assigned his new pastoral associate to be chaplain of the parish's women's Bible study group. After meeting with the women for the first time, the young associate staggered back to the rectory.

"What's wrong?" the pastor asked her.

"It was terrible," she said. "All they talked about were their aches and pains, their children's sickness and their husbands' cholesterol, heart, and prostate woes. It wasn't a Bible class; it was an organ recital."

The mother superior of the local convent was rushing to a meeting when she blew through a red light and was flagged down by a young cop. He quickly recognized the nun from his days attending Catholic school.

"You know, Sister," he told her, "you just drove through a red light. I'll let it go this time, but you'll have to be very careful at the next intersection."

"Thank you, my son," said the nun and asked, "Is that one a very dangerous intersection?"

"You bet, Sister," replied the cop. "The cop on duty there is a Methodist."

———

The driver for a local dry cleaner got a kick out of pulling up in front of the convent every week and loudly shouting out: Hey, girls, got any dirty habits?"

———

A couple of good ol' Catholic boys were out fishing on a Sunday morning. One of them was feeling a bit guilty about missing Mass.

The other was unconcerned. "I couldn't have gone anyway," he said. "The golf course is closed for a private tournament."

Seamus always had a fondness for beer and it was causing trouble in his marriage. The pastor thought about how to begin a conversation with him about the problem.

One Sunday the priest caught Seamus as he was slipping out of church after communion and dragged him into a corner. He asked him, "Why is it, Seamus, that every Sunday, even before Mass is over, you head straight for the local bar?"

"Well, Father," said Seamus, "think about it this way: it's what you might call my 'thirst after righteousness.'"

Whenever he preached, the new associate pastor worked out a little system with the pastor. The pastor would stand in the sacristy, just out of sight of the congregation and signal the preacher about his homily.

If he rubbed his hand over his hair it was a signal that the associate pastor was talking over peoples' heads. Other signals worked the same way: touching his ear meant he should speak more loudly; a finger across her neck meant he was talking too long.

One Sunday, the preacher really got into his homily and neglected to glance over at the pastor. Finally, after more than 20 minutes he finally looked toward the sacristy door.

And saw the pastor frantically holding his nose.

It was a terrible flight. There was lightning all around the plane, which was bouncing like a rubber ball through the turbulent air. The passenger was comforted by the fact that his seatmate was a nun, habit and all.

Finally, the man could stand no more of the frightening ride. He turned to the nun and pleaded: "Sister, can't you do something?"

Her own knuckles white from grasping the armrests, she replied, "I'm afraid not; I'm in sales, not management."

———

It was his first homily after ordination and the deacon was very nervous. It got worse when he noticed that members of the congregation didn't seem to be paying attention. Finally, he stopped his homily and asked, "Can you all hear me in the back?"

A parishioner called out, "Not really!"

Which was followed by everyone in the front of the church getting up and moving to the rear.

———

Two members of the parish council were discussing their pastor's preaching. "His homilies are like chickens with their heads cut off," one said. "Whenever you think his homily is done, it just jumps back up and heads off in another direction."

As soon as he was assigned to a small rural parish, the priest was faced with a crisis: several of the leading members of the parish died. He was so overwhelmed by the number of back-to-back funerals that he wasn't able to prepare a new homily for three weeks. He just used the one from the week before over and over again.

Members of the parish council were upset by this and contacted the bishop. "What was the homily about?" the bishop asked the council members. When no one could tell him, the bishop smiled and said, ""Maybe Father had better use it one more time."

The director of St. Mary's ministry to the homeless spotted one of the clients panhandling near the church. He seemed to be much worse off than usual. So she took a $20 bill from her purse, slipped it into an envelope, and wrote in large letters, "PERSEVERE!" Then she dropped it unobtrusively at the man's feet. He picked it up, read the note, and smiled thankfully.

The next night, the man came into the shelter and slipped the director a huge wad of bills.

"What's this?" the director asked him.

"You were right," the man said. "Persevere came in first at the track yesterday and paid 30-1. This is your half of the winnings."

It was a gorgeous Sunday. The weather was perfect and the pastor could see that his congregation was just itching for Mass to get over with so they could get on with their day outdoors. So he told them: "You get to choose my homily today. I have a $5,000 one that lasts two minutes; a $1,000 one that takes 20 minutes; and a $100 homily that takes an hour."

The people looked at one another, and then the pastor said, "Before I begin, let's take up the collection first."

Little Janie really didn't like going to Mass. One Sunday her parents tried a small bribe. If Janie wouldn't raise a fuss in church they would take her to her favorite restaurant afterwards.

During his spirited homily about the choice between heaven and hell, the priest demanded, "And where are those who live good and just lives going to go?"

Janie blurted out, "If you ever get done, to my favorite restaurant!"

One of his parishioners was a powerful politician who was always trying to ingratiate himself with the pastor. One Sunday, the politician asked the priest, "Just tell me what the government can do to help the church?"

The pastor's quick reply: "Stop making $1 bills."

The priest was a good driver, but he had a heavy foot. His collar usually could get him out of a ticket, but this time the motorcycle cop was adamant. The priest said to him, "Blessed are the merciful for they shall obtain mercy."

As he slapped the ticket into the priest's hand, the cop smiled and said, "Go, and sin no more."

**The best prayer: "Lord, make me
the kind of person my dog thinks I am."**

**The worst prayer: "Lord, make me
the kind of person my cat wants me to be."**

The catechist began her lesson with a question. "Boys and girls, what do we know about God?"

Little Jonnie's hand shot up. "He's an artist."

"Really," said the teacher. "And just how do you know that?"

"It easy," said Jonnie. "Our Father, who does art in heaven…"

His mom asked Little Jonnie, "How do you expect to get into heaven when you're always acting up?"

Jonnie thought for a minute and replied, "Well, I'll just run in and out and in and out and keep slamming the door until St. Peter says, 'For heaven's sake, Jonnie, either come in or stay out!'"

It was Cemetery Sunday and Angelina Lupo decided to visit the grave of her late husband Vincent, a retired mobster, for the first time to say a little prayer over him. But when Angelina arrived at Resurrection Cemetery she couldn't find poor Vinnie's gravesite. Finally, she came across a groundskeeper who ushered her into a small room where the records were kept.

Poring over maps and lists, he finally turned to the widow and said, "I can find no record of a Vincent Lupo buried here. The closest I can find is an Angelina Lupo."

"That's him," she cried. "He always put everything in my name."

It was Little Jonnie's first time at Mass. He watched earnestly as ushers passed around the long-handled baskets at the offertory.

When they neared his family's pew, Jonnie said loudly, "Don't pay for me, Daddy, I'm under five."

The woman was making the family's traditional Easter ham, just as her mother and her grandmother had done for generations. Her young daughter, eager to understand the family traditions, watched as her mother sliced off the ends of the ham before placing it in the roasting pan.

"Mom," asked the girl, "why are you doing that?"

Her mother paused for a moment and then said, "You know, I'm not sure. But this is the way I always saw my mother make a ham. Let's call Grandma and ask her."

So, she phoned her mother and asked why they always slice the ends off the ham before baking it.

The grandmother pondered for a moment and said, "You know, I'm not sure why, but this is how *my* mother always made it."

Now everyone was very curious. So off they all went to visit great-grandmother in the nursing home.

They asked her, "Grandma, you know when we make an Easter ham we always slice off the ends before baking it. Why is that?"

"I don't know why *you* do it," said the old woman, "but I never had a pan that was large enough!"

Q: What does the B-I-B-L-E stand for?

A: Basic Information Before Leaving Earth.

A priest had an important appointment with the bishop downtown but couldn't find a parking spot. Because he was late he finally took a chance and left his car in a no-parking zone.

He put a note under the windshield wiper that read: "I have circled the block 10 times. If I don't park here, I'll miss my appointment with the bishop. Forgive us our trespasses."

When he returned two hours later, he found a parking ticket and a note from the beat cop. It read, "I've circled this block for 10 years. If I don't give you a ticket I'll lose my job. Lead us not into temptation."

Sunday after Mass, Mom asked Little Janie what she learned from her religious ed class.

The girl replied, "Don't be scared and you'll get your quilt."

Of course Mom was puzzled. Later in the day, she ran into the catechist who taught her daughter's class and asked what that day's lesson was about.

"Be not afraid," she said, "your Comforter is coming."

You know how some people just don't have a grasp of the obvious? One pastor was upset when the building fund drive came up short. He got up in the pulpit on Sunday and announced, "I have bad news. Someone has stolen $200,000 in pledges!"

The Catholic doctor, known for his successful treatment of the lame, had a waiting room full of people when a little old woman, completely bent over, shuffled in slowly leaning on her cane. When her turn came, she went into the doctor's office, and, amazingly, emerged minutes later walking erect with her head held high.

Another patient who also was waiting went up to the little old lady and proclaimed, "A miracle! It's a miracle! You walked in bent in half and now you're walking erect. What did that doctor do?"

The little old lady answered, "Miracle, shmiracle. He gave me a longer cane."

The old pastor had a very small church in a very rural diocese in the western U.S. He was a thin man who always had a smile for people. He also owned a horse; it was his only indulgence and a blessing for his rural ministry.

One day a visitor asked him, "Father, how come you're so thin while your horse is fat?"

With a twinkle, the old priest replied. "Because I feed the horse and my parish feeds me."

**There are four "tire brands" among Catholics:
the tireless, the tired, the retired, and the tiresome.**

At a Catholic Charities staff development meeting, a nutrition expert was proclaiming the values of good eating. "The stuff we regularly put into our stomachs is enough to have killed most of us several times over," said the outspoken nutritionist. "Red meat is awful. Soft drinks corrode your stomach lining. Most of our foods are loaded with salt. High-fat diets can be disastrous, and none of us realizes the long-term harm caused by the bacteria in our drinking water."

The audience was startled, obviously made uncomfortable by the nutritionist's words.

"But there is one food that is the most dangerous of all," he continued, "and most of us have eaten it or will eat it. Would anyone care to guess what food causes the most grief and suffering for years after eating it?"

The room was quiet. Finally, in the front row, a Catholic Charities marriage counselor raised her hand and said, "Wedding cake?"

It was a great day for a great Irish Catholic wedding when Mike Murphy and Maureen Muldoon tied the knot. Everyone in the village was there. To kick things off at the reception, the DJ yelled, "OK now, will all you married guys go stand next to the one person who has made your life worth living."

All the men went and stood next to their moms.

A missionary nun was flying to her new assignment, a remote mission in Alaska's bush country, with a pilot of a small plane. She was the only passenger.

Suddenly the pilot grasped his chest and slumped over. Frantically, the nun grabbed the radio and yelled, "Mayday! Mayday! This is Sister Susan. Help me! Help me! My pilot had a heart attack and I don't know how to fly. I'm alone in the plane! Help me! Please help me!"

A voice came over the radio. "This is Air Traffic Control and I have you loud and clear, Sister. I'll talk you through this and get you back on the ground safely. I've had a lot of experience with this kind of problem. Everything will be fine. Now give me your altitude and location."

She says, "I'm 5-foot 4-inches tall and I'm in the front seat."

"OK," says the voice on the radio. "Repeat after me: 'Our Father, who art in heaven...'"

One day, the boss asked one of his frequently absent employees, "Do you believe in life after death?"

"Why, yes, in fact I do," replied the employee.

"Well then, that makes everything just fine," the boss went on. "Because after you left early yesterday to go to your grandmother's funeral, she stopped in to see you!"

A single guy was pretty lonely. He decided life would be more fun if he had a pet. So he went to the pet store and told the owner that he wanted to buy a pet that was, well, a bit different. The owner suggested his most unusual and unique pet, a talking centipede. The little bug even came with a little white box he lived in.

At home, the man decided he would start things off by taking his new companion to church. So he asked the centipede in the box, "Would you like to go to church with me today? We'll have a great time."

But there was no answer from his new pet.

This bothered him a bit, and after a few minutes he asked again, "How about going to church with me to receive blessings?"

But again, no answer came from the little white box.

More than a little concerned, the man waited a few more minutes and then decided to make one more invitation.

This time he put his face up against the centipede's house and shouted, "Hey, in there! Would you like to go to church with me and learn about God?"

Finally, a little voice came out of the box. "I heard you the first time! I'm putting my shoes on."

———

Responding to a mailing about supporting the parish's building fund, a man told his pastor: "You know I'll give 'til it hurts. But you also need to know that I'm very sensitive to pain."

One Easter Sunday morning as the priest was preaching at a special children's liturgy, he reached into his pocket and pulled out an egg. He pointed at the egg and asked the children, "What's in here?"

"I know," Little Janie shouted out. "Pantyhose!"

———

The deacon was doing some "unofficial" premarital counseling with his daughter and her fiancé. He asked, "Young man, can you support a family?"

The surprised groom-to-be replied, "Well, no. I was just planning to support your daughter. The rest of you will have to fend for yourselves."

———

Like many priests, this one loved his golf. On a vacation he had the opportunity to play at a course where Tiger Woods often teed up. At one of the more challenging holes, the priest's caddie told him, "When Tiger plays this hole he uses a two-iron and always says a prayer."

"That's good advice," said the priest and pulled out a two-iron. He said a prayer, but nevertheless his shot hooked into the rough. "I guess the Lord didn't hear my prayer," he said dejectedly.

"Oh, he probably heard you," said the caddie. "But when Tiger prays, he keeps his head down."

In his ministry at the local jail, the deacon was fond of showing off his knowledge of the Bible by quoting verses to prisoners. Meeting with an inmate accused of stealing automobiles, the deacon said to him, "When you were tempted by that shiny new sports car, why didn't you just say, 'Get thee behind me, Satan'?"

The prisoner looked up and said dolefully, "I did; I did. But Satan replied that it didn't matter who went first, since we were both headed in the same direction."

———

The small town's newspaper always placed the titles of upcoming sermons and homilies from the community's churches. On Monday, the pastor of St. Mary's emailed the paper's editor. "Thank you very much," he wrote, "for the error you made in the paper last week. The homily title I sent was, 'Jesus and the Publican.' You printed it as 'Jesus and the Republicans' and we had an overflow crowd at Mass."

———

Two "church ladies" were comparing notes about their parishes. One said, "My pastor is so good he can preach on any subject for an hour."

To which the other replied, "That's nothing. Mine can talk for an hour on nothing at all."

Old Miss Gladys was a fixture in the front pew of St. Matthew's Church, always quick to greet visitors with a hearty welcome.

This particular Sunday, the deacon's homily went on and on; even Gladys was a bit bored. Still, after Mass she spotted a newcomer and went up to him. "Hello," she said brightly, "I'm Gladys Dunn."

The visitor yawned and said, "You're not the only one."

The mother rushed into the bedroom and shouted to her husband: "Quick! Call the emergency room, Little Jonnie just swallowed a quarter!"

The husband sighed and said, "Just call the pastor. He can get money out of anyone."

The order priest giving the parish mission was very good and very much sought-after. As a result, he had a bit of an ego. In the midst of one of his talks, he mentioned offhandedly that his order had insured his voice for a million dollars.

Unimpressed, one woman at the coffee hour afterwards went up to the priest and asked him, "So, what did the order do with the proceeds?"

Slogans for the building fund brochure:

- Give generously, according to what you reported on your income tax.
- Give now, before the cost of living goes up and you can't afford it.
- It's more blessed to give than to receive; it's also tax-deductible.
- The Lord loves a cheerful giver; but he'll accept money from a grouch.
- You can't take your money with you, but you can send it on ahead."

If the Magi were three wise women they would have arrived on time, helped deliver the baby, cleaned the stable, made a casserole, and made their gift a year's supply of disposable diapers.

The religious education teacher was telling the little children about the Advent wreath. After explaining the meaning of the purple candles, she asked, "Can anyone tell me what the pink one means?"

Little Jonnie's hand shot up and he said, knowingly: "Sure! They're expecting a girl."

A deacon who constantly struggled with his weight wasn't quite sure what to think when he received two boxes of Christmas treats from a parishioner.

The note read: "I know you don't eat sweets, so I am sending the candy to your wife and nuts to you."

The priest was reading the wedding vows to the nervous bridegroom: "Do you take this woman to be your wedded wife, for better or worse, for richer or poorer, in sickness…"

"Stop, Father," interrupted the bride. "You're going to talk him out of it."

The frustrated music minister was trying to start a handbell choir but was hamstrung by one participant who couldn't quite get it.

"No, no," the woman told the choir member, "it's ding before dong except after bong."

Betcha didn't know that Noah was quite the punster. After loading all the animals on the ark, he quipped, "Now I've herd everything."

After her first religious education class in a new town after moving from Minneapolis to New Orleans, Little Janie came home upset. "I'm not going to class ever again," she pouted.

Her mother, clearly curious, asked, "Why?"

"They were talking all about St. Paul but never once mentioned Minneapolis."

———

It was going to be an exciting day. For the first time Little Jonnie was going to see a baby get baptized at Mass. He watched very carefully, especially when the deacon scooped up water and poured it on the child's head.

Aghast, Jonnie turned to his mother and asked in loud voice, "Mommy, why is he waterboarding that baby?"

———

The bishop just hired a new secretary for the chancery office.

She previously worked for the Pentagon.

Now the bishop's filing system goes from "Sacred" to "Top Sacred."

The substitute teacher at St. Mary's Catholic School needed supplies to teach her class. But the cabinet was locked and she couldn't recall the combination the principal had rattled off to her that morning.

Finally, she spotted the pastor wandering through the school visiting classrooms. She pulled him into the supply room and asked if he could help. The priest made a couple of attempts at the combination and then looked toward heaven. Finally, as his lips moved silently he turned the lock to the final numbers and it clicked open.

The teacher was impressed. "Your faith is so strong," she gushed.

"Not so," replied the pastor, pointing upward. "The combination is written on a piece of paper taped to the ceiling."

When Jesus went into the region of Caesarea Philippi he asked his disciples, "Who do people say that the Son of Man is?" They replied, "Some say John the Baptist, others Elijah, still others Jeremiah or one of the prophets." He said to them, "But who do you say that I am?"

Simon Peter said in reply, "Master, you are the supreme eschatological manifestation of omnipotent ecclesiastical authority, the absolute, divine and sacerdotal monarch."

And Jesus said, "Huh?"

The small town's only barber was a negative, arrogant, know-it-all. When one of his regular clients mentioned that he had just returned from Rome where he'd had a chance to meet the Pope, the barber scoffed.

"Don't make me laugh," the barber snorted. "Why would the Pope meet with you? I bet you just saw him from his balcony with all the rest of the crowd."

"Not so," retorted the customer. "We were in St. Peter's Square with everyone else, but suddenly two Swiss Guards showed up and told me the Pope wanted to see me privately."

"I'll bet," said the barber.

"It's true," insisted the man. "The guards whisked me into the Pope's private apartment for a meeting."

"What did the Pope say?" asked the barber incredulously.

"He wanted to know who gave me such a terrible haircut."

Not long after his ordination, the newly-minted deacon learned just how impressed his young son was with his new role. "Dad," he said, "I've decided that I want to become a great preacher just like you so that I can help clean up the mess we've made of this world!"

"That's really great, son," the deacon replied. "Why don't go upstairs and start with your room?"

Like many newly ordained deacons, John threw himself into parish activities and work with abandon. He frequently told parishioners that if they wanted a pastoral visit to just drop him an email and he would stop by.

One night, checking his email before yet another meeting, John received a note reading, "I am one of your loneliest parishioners and biggest contributors. May I have a visit tomorrow evening?"

It was signed by his wife.

——

The drought in parts of the county had gotten so bad that churches were forced to temporarily change the ways in which they celebrated baptism.

The Baptists took up sprinkling, the Catholics used damp cloths, and the Methodists gave out rain checks.

——

The hard-of-hearing liturgist was writing down the petitions for Sunday Mass when a parishioner dashed in and said, "I'm in a hurry, but can you please ask for prayers for my biopsy next week?"

The liturgist agreed and scribbled down the request. At Mass, the reader intoned the petitions, asking everyone to "pray for Mrs. Brown's autopsy."

If it's true that absence makes the heart grow fonder, then lots of Catholics sure love their parish.

———

The pastor was preaching on forgiveness and the sacrament of reconciliation. He made a point of saying that the sacrament also meant that to be forgiven meant you were to forgive others. After Mass, a very elderly woman tottered up to him and said, "You know, I can't forgive my enemies."

"And why not?" demanded the pastor.

"I don't have any," she replied.

"Now that's quite unusual," pressed the priest. "Just how did you manage to accomplish that?"

The woman answered, "It was easy. I've outlived them all."

———

St. Raphael Parish was celebrating its 100th anniversary. The parish had invited several former pastors and the diocesan bishop to concelebrate Mass. Afterward in the parish hall, the pastor called a group of children together to talk about the importance of the anniversary. He began by introducing the bishop and asking the children, "Can anyone tell me what a bishop does?"

There was silence. But finally, Little Janie in the back piped up and said, "I think he moves diagonally."

During daily Mass, the celebrant usually gave the congregation the opportunity to offer petitions. There were the usual petitions for the sick, for service members overseas and the like. Finally, a man stood and said, "My grandson got his driver's license yesterday. Let us pray for us all."

In his homily about death, the priest said, "You know, every member of St. Raphael's parish is going to die someday."

Then he spotted a man in a back pew chuckling. So the priest shouted all the louder, "You know, every member of this church is going to die someday."

This caused the man to break out in a full belly laugh. The priest was distracted but nevertheless finished his homily.

After Mass, he sought out the man and asked what he had said that made him laugh so hard.

The man answered with a grin, "I belong to St. Joseph's parish."

The head of the parish council met with the pastor and said, "Father, the council has some advice for you…"

Interrupting, the pastor said, "The trouble with you people's advice is that it usually interferes with my plans."

A couple of friends were discussing the deacon's preaching. "Well," said one, "at least he always seems to have a surprise ending."

"What surprises me," answered another, "is that just when you think it's about to end, it doesn't."

ABOUT THE AUTHORS

Deacon Tom Sheridan

As a veteran secular newspaperman, Tom Sheridan developed a keen eye for the humor in life. A deacon ordained in 1979 for the Diocese of Joliet, Illinois, and a former editor of the Archdiocese of Chicago's newspaper and other publications, Deacon Tom also knows a little about the humor to be found in religion. And as a husband and father of five children and several grandchildren, he believes humor will help see us all through our various struggles. He writes from Ocala, Florida, where he lives with his wife, Kathy. He is the author of *The Book of Catholic Jokes*, *The Gift of Baptism*, and *The Gift of Godparents* for ACTA Publications.

Sister Mary Kathleen Glavich

Sister Mary Kathleen Glavich, a Sister of Notre Dame from Cleveland, Ohio, is an author, editor, and speaker. For more than thirty years, she has produced faith formation materials including more than seventy books, such as the Catholic Companion series (ACTA Publications). Her latest is a debut novel, *The Fisherman's Wife: The Gospel According to St. Peter's Spouse*. Sister Kathleen is known to spice her talks with jokes, and her blog's homepage (www.kathleenglavich.org) contains "SND School Humor." Three times she has ventured to Dubai to speak at religious conferences. (No joke!)

Also Available from ACTA Publications

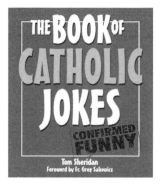

The Book of Catholic Jokes

Deacon Tom Sheridan
Foreword by Fr. Greg Sakowicz

96 pages, paperback (#148), $10.95,
978-0-87946-377-9

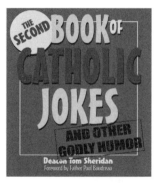

The Second Book of Catholic Jokes

Deacon Tom Sheridan
Foreword by Fr. Paul Boudreau

96 pages, paperback (#1038), $10.95,
978-0-87946-425-7

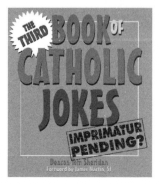

The Third Book of Catholic Jokes

Deacon Tom Sheridan
Foreword by Fr. James Martin, SJ

96 pages, paperback (#1050), $10.95,
978-0-87946-461-5

www.actapublications.com 800-397-2282